This book is dedicated to all the children
who think that they are different from the rest of their families.
Just remember your family loves you just the way you are.

One cold night, twelve piglets were born in a barn.

LITTLE PINK PUP

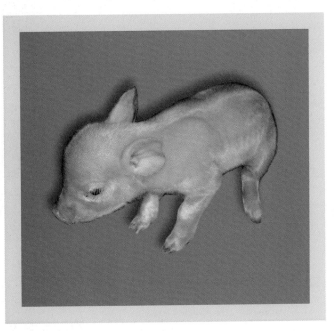

Johanna Kerby

SCHOLASTIC INC.
New York Toronto London Auckland
Sydney Mexico City New Delhi Hong Kong

ISBN 978-0-545-45950-1

12 11 10 9 8 7 6 5 4 3 2 1   12 13 14 15 16 17/0

Printed in the U.S.A.   40

First Scholastic printing, January 2012

Design by Marikka Tamura
Text set in Avenir

The smallest one
was named Pink.

Pink's brother and sister piglets
were strong and healthy, but
he was tiny and weak.

They were playful and pushed Pink
aside when it was time to eat.

Pink was cold and hungry.
His owners brought him into
their house to see if they
could help Pink.

Tink was a brand-new dachshund mom.
She had one puppy of her own and was
a foster mom to a few others.

When Tink saw Pink, she
immediately welcomed
him into the family.

She licked him and fed him
and tucked him in close.

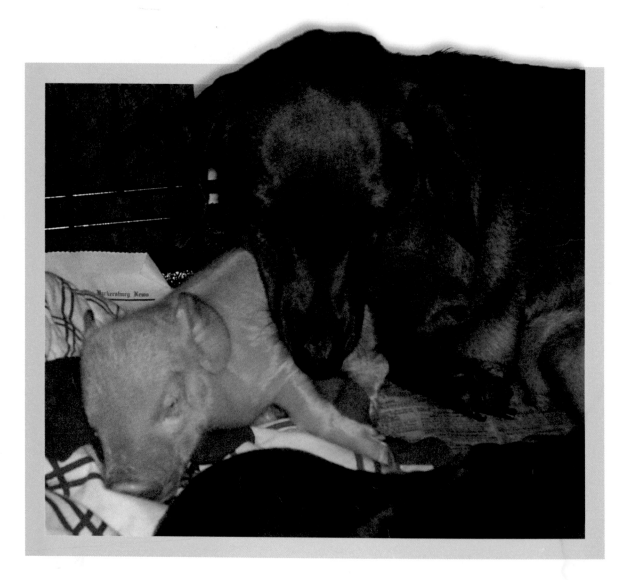

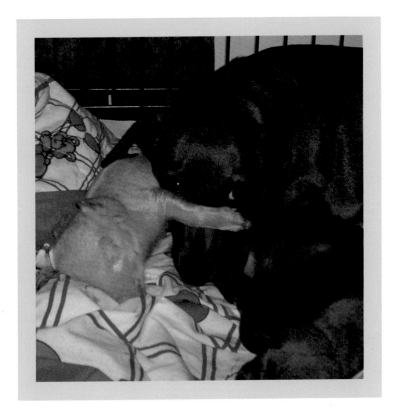

She made him feel
right at home.

Tink knew that Pink was different from
her puppies. But she didn't mind.

Now Tink had lots of brown
puppies and one little pink pup.

Pink's new siblings welcomed him, too. He may not have looked like them, but that didn't matter. He was just their size!

The puppies didn't sleep on straw like the pigs in the barn.

They slept on a soft blanket, and their warm bodies kept Pink cozy.

Little by little, Pink started to eat more.

Nobody pushed him away.

He began to grow stronger, along with his puppy siblings.

Soon Pink was running
around the house.

They liked to wrestle and nip at each other.

They chased each other
and played tag.

Pink loved to get his ears scratched. But he hated taking a bath! When it was bath time, he would squeal loudly and kick out his legs.

Sometimes Pink would visit his pig family in the barn. His pig siblings had grown so big!

They were about twenty pounds each, and Pink weighed only three pounds.

After his visit, Pink was always happy
to go back to Tink and his dog family.

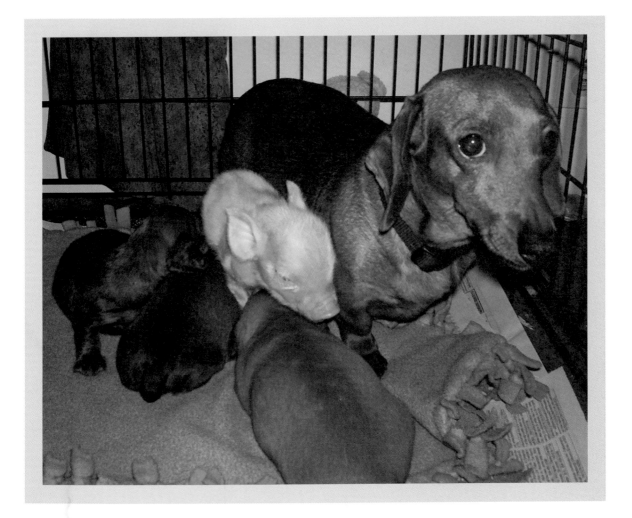

Once Pink and the puppies
got a little older, it was time
to eat solid food.

But when Pink was offered
pig food, he refused to eat.

He wanted puppy
food like his brothers
and sisters!

When Pink got too big to live in
the house, he moved into the barn—

—but he made sure to take
his dog bed with him.

After sleeping on a soft cushion his whole
life, he did not like the scratchy straw.

The dogs missed Pink.

But they would still play
with him in the barn.

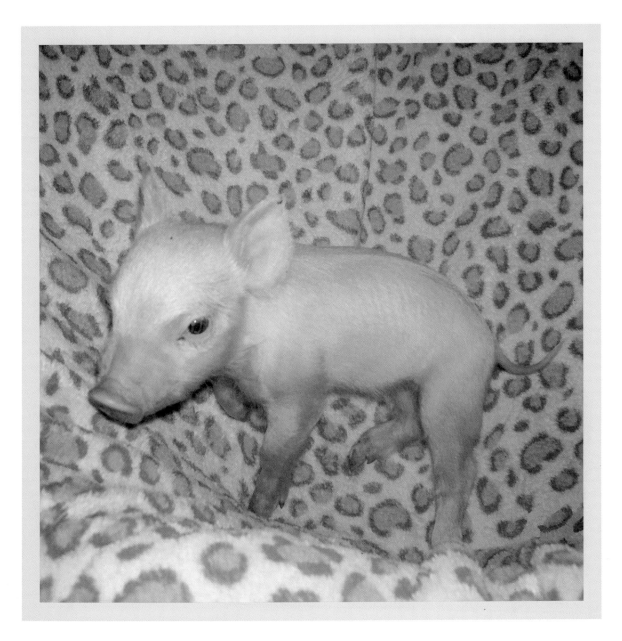

Our family lives on a small farm where we raise pigs, horses, goats, dogs and cats. We particularly love pigs for their personalities and enjoy just watching them root around the pen. My four children raise pigs for 4-H, a program dedicated to providing hands-on education for youth across America by learning leadership, citizenship and life skills.

The highlight of every spring is when a new litter of pigs is born. Last year, our sow delivered twelve piglets. One of the piglets was premature, so we brought him inside and one of our dachshunds became his foster mom. When we put some photos on the Internet, people from all over the country contacted us and we knew their story was special. Dachshunds are known for being good mothers, and they are also very sweet and funny. It is amazing how much compassion and love an animal can have for not only their own babies, but a baby from a completely different species. Thanks to Tink's love, Pink is thriving on the farm today.

I would like to thank my family, friends and all those who encouraged me to write this book.

Johanna Kerby

Johanna Kerby
Elizabeth, West Virginia